Melissa Davis

BENNIE THE FLYING SQUIRREL

tate publishing
CHILDREN'S DIVISION

Bennie the Flying Squirrel
Copyright © 2016 by Melissa Davis. All rights reserved.

This title is also available as a Tate Out Loud product. Visit www.tatepublishing.com for more information.

No part of this publication may be reproduced, stored in a retrieval system or transmitted in any way by any means, electronic, mechanical, photocopy, recording or otherwise without the prior permission of the author except as provided by USA copyright law.

The opinions expressed by the author are not necessarily those of Tate Publishing, LLC.

This novel is a work of fiction. Names, descriptions, entities, and incidents included in the story are products of the author's imagination. Any resemblance to actual persons, events, and entities is entirely coincidental.

Published by Tate Publishing & Enterprises, LLC
127 E. Trade Center Terrace | Mustang, Oklahoma 73064 USA
1.888.361.9473 | www.tatepublishing.com

Tate Publishing is committed to excellence in the publishing industry. The company reflects the philosophy established by the founders, based on Psalm 68:11,
"The Lord gave the word and great was the company of those who published it."

Book design copyright © 2016 by Tate Publishing, LLC. All rights reserved.
Cover and interior design by Eileen Cueno
Illustrations by Patrick Bucoy

Published in the United States of America

ISBN: 978-1-68097-280-1
1. Family / Relationships
2. Nature / General
16.07.08

THIS BOOK BELONGS TO:

_____

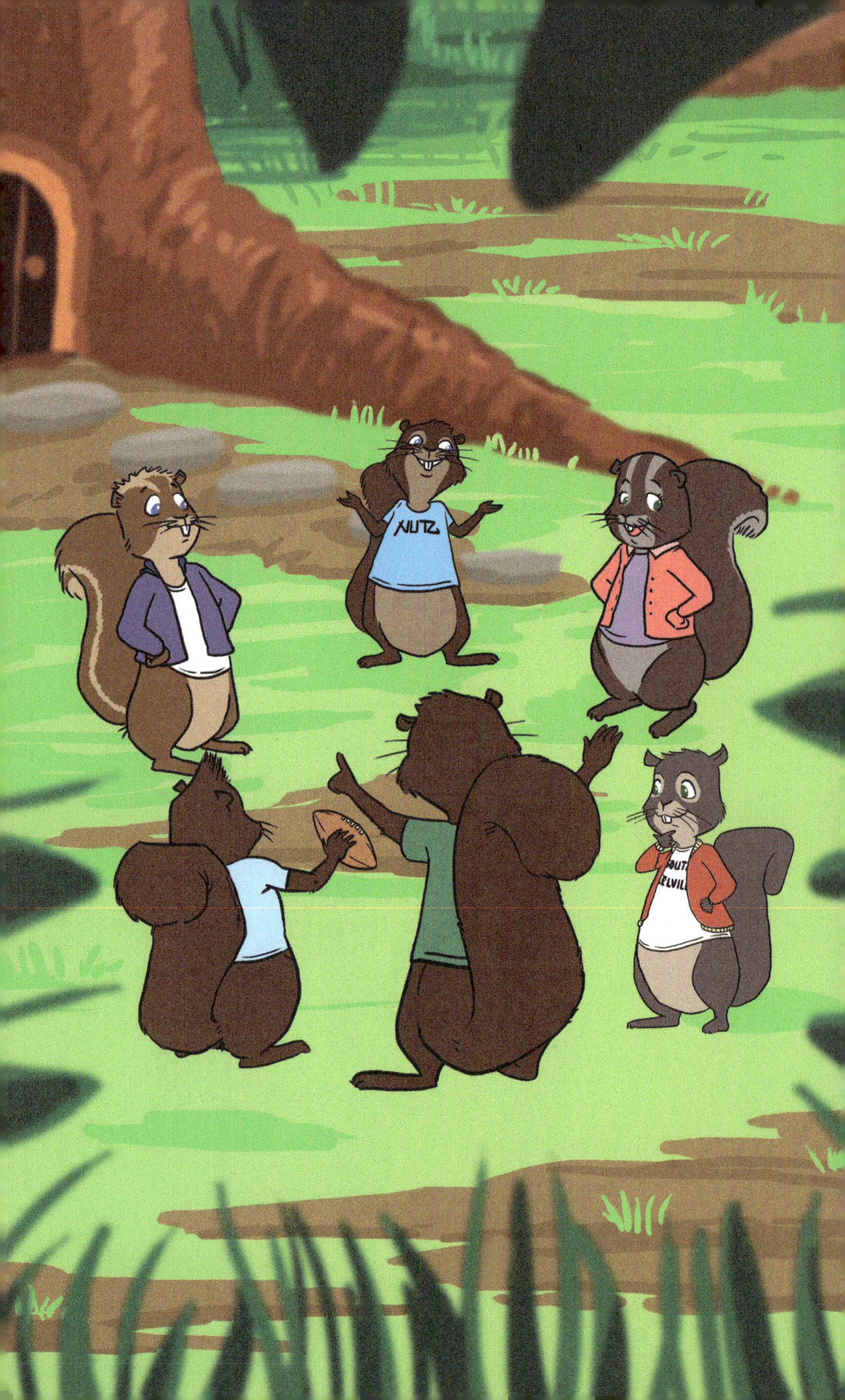
NUTZ

ON A BRIGHT SUNNY DAY IN THE WOODS A SQUIRREL NAMED BENNIE WAS PLAYING WITH HIS BROTHERS AND SISTER. THEY WERE ALL TALKING ABOUT SOMEWHERE ELSE BESIDES SOUTH SQUIRRELVILLE. DREAMING ABOUT THE CITY AND WHAT IT WOULD BE LIKE TO GO VISIT IT. THE CITY WAS ALWAYS A DREAM OF BENNIE'S SINCE HE WAS LITTLE. AS THEY WERE ALL SITTING AROUND TALKING, MARCO SAID, HOW COOL IT WOULD BE TO SEE ALL THOSE SPORTS CARS AND TO SEE HOW FAST THEY CAN GO. ROSA SAID, WHAT IT WOULD BE LIKE TO LIVE SO CLOSE TO OTHER HOUSES AND HAVE NEIGHBORS. ANTONIO SAID, I GOT THIS! I AM GOING TO TRAVEL ALL OVER THE WORLD ONE DAY. DONATO SAID, YOU SILLY SQUIRRELS YOU DO NOT HAVE TO DREAM ABOUT LEAVING THIS PLACE. YOU HAVE EVERYTHING HERE IN SOUTH SQUIRRELVILLE. AND I AM GOING TO SETTLE DOWN AND MARRY ISABELLA. EVERYONE LAUGHED. FELIPE SAID , I JUST WANT TO PLAY SPORTS FOR THE REST OF MY LIFE. GO SQUIRRELS! GO SQUIRRELS!! ROSA SAID, YOU ARE SUCH A SILLY, SILLY SQUIRREL.

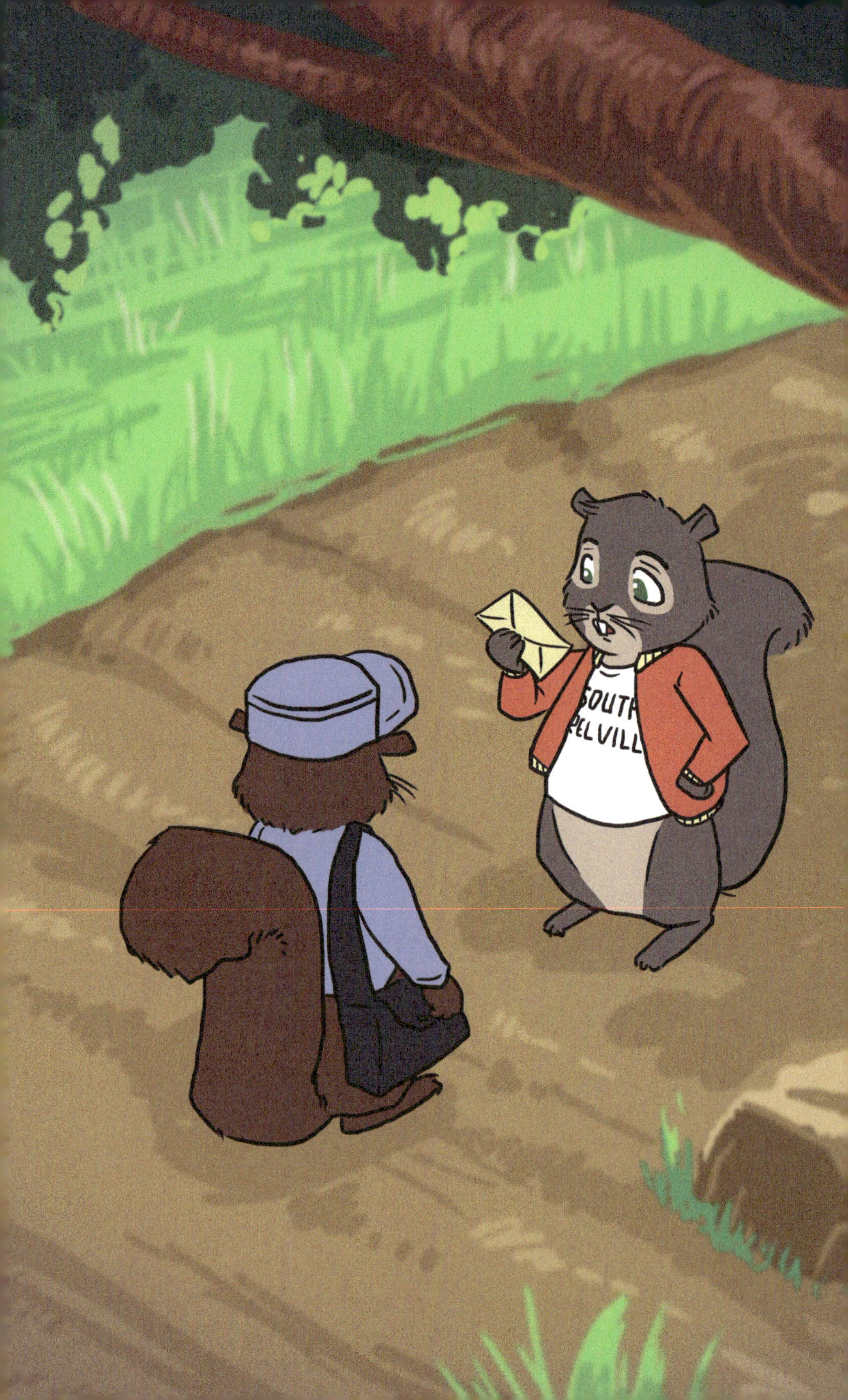

COMING DOWN THE ROAD WAS MR. SANTINI THE MAILMAN. HE SAID YOU HAVE MAIL! EVERYONE RAN TO GO SEE WHO SENT THE MAIL TO THEM. BENNIE OPENED THE LETTER SO FAST AND LOOKED AT HIS FAMILY. THE LETTER WAS FROM HIS COUSIN VINNY IN THE CITY. THE LETTER SAID, DEAR FAMILY, I AM WRITING TO TELL YOU THAT I AM IN TROUBLE. PLEASE COME SOON TO HELP! EVERYONE LOOKED AT ONE ANOTHER AND SAID BENNIE, YOU HAVE TO GO AND HELP! BENNIE SAID WHY ME? THEY SAID YOU ARE THE CLOSEST TO HIM AND YOU WILL KNOW WHAT TO DO. BENNIE SAID IM SCARED TO GO TO THE CITY BY MYSELF. BENNIE WALKED AWAY FROM HIS FAMILY AND WAS HITTING AN ACORN DOWN THE ROAD.

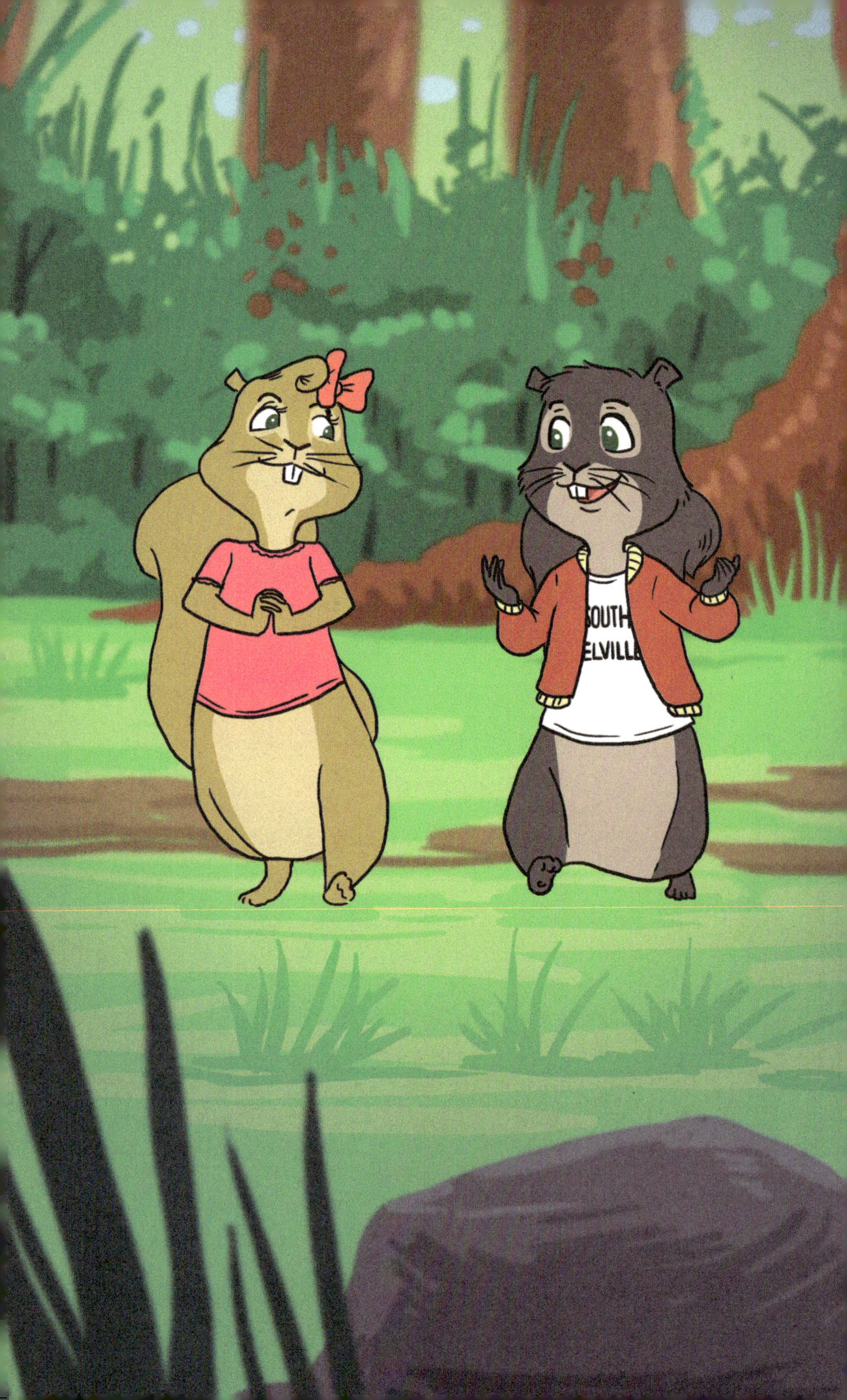
SOUTH
ELVILLE

Around the corner was Isabella. And she was playing with her brother Bennie she said. Well hey stranger! Isabella said hey Bennie! What have you been up to? Bennie said im flying out tomorrow to the city to help my cousin Vinny out. Isabella said why do you look so sad? He said im nervous about flying so far away. I have no direction, no map and no address to find my cousin Vinny. Isabella said. Bennie you are the smartest squirrel with the biggest heart that I know. I know when you put your mind to something, you will accomplish this task for your family. I have confidence in you! Bennie said, thank you! I can always rely on you to reinsure me on anything. She smiled and said, ill see you when you return and Isabella waved to him. He looked at her for a minute while she was playing with a acorn with her brother. He smiled and continued to kick an acorn down the road. He thought to himself, how am I going to get there. It's a huge city! He was nervous and felt like he had too much responsibility on his shoulders.

BUT THEN HE REMEMBERED WHAT ISABELLA SAID TO HIM AND HE SAID, IM GOING TO FLY TO THE CITY AND MAKE THIS HAPPEN FOR MY FAMILY. THE NEXT DAY HE WAS LOOKING AROUND IN THE BARN AND HE NOTICED THAT HIS DAD USED TO GO FLYING WHEN HE WAS YOUNGER WITH THESE SPECIAL WINGS. BENNIE SAID, THAT'S WHAT I NEED TO GO FIND MY COUSIN VINNY. BENNIE GATHERED HIS WHOLE FAMILY AROUND TO DO SOME PRACTICING WITH THE WINGS. HE PRACTICED SEVERAL TIMES JUMPING OFF THE HILL UNTIL HE FELT COMFORTABLE ENOUGH TO DO IT FOR SEVERAL MILES ALONE. HIS FAMILY ENCOURAGED HIM THAT IF HE PUTS HIS MIND TO ANYTHING IN THIS WORLD THAT THEY KNEW HE COULD DO IT. BENNIE PACKED THAT NIGHT AND PLACED EVERYTHING IN ONE BACKPACK. MOM MADE FOOD SO HE WOULD NOT GO HUNGRY FOR HIS TRIP TO THE CITY. THE NEXT DAY BENNIE GOT UP REAL EARLY TO HEAD OUT TO HIS ADVENTURE TO THE CITY. HE WAVED AND SMILED AND HE FLEW UP IN THE AIR. AS BENNIE WAS FLYING HE NOTICED HE COULD SEE SO MUCH FROM THE SKY. HE WAS SO AMAZED! HE FLEW OVER MOUNTAINS AND DEEP WATERS. AS HE WAS TRAVELING HE CAME ACROSS A BIRD THAT WAS IN FRONT OF HIM. HE GOT A LITTLE CLOSER AND INTRODUCED HIMSELF TO THE BIRD.

The bird looked at him and said well hello my name is Three Can Sam! Bennie looked at him and said wow! What a name. Where are you from? Three Cam Sam said, I'm from West Squirrelville and I'm flying to the big city to watch the Squirrelnals play today. Bennie said, I'm going to the city as well. Can I fly with you? Three Cam Sam said absolutely! Bennie said how did you get that name? Three Cam Sam said when I was born I had three cameraman taking my picture and my mom named me Sam, so they called me 3 Cam Sam. Bennie just laughed. Only in the west! As they were flying they were talking about how the city was so amazing with great food and entertainment. Three Cam Sam said you know they have the best Italian food in the city. Bennie said I have heard that from my cousin Vinny in the past. Three Cam Sam said well here we are! Look at those bright lights and those landmarks everywhere. Bennie smiled and Three Cam Sam said I'm off to the see the game! Bennie said to Three Cam Sam...Go Squirrelnals! Three Cam Sam said be careful and enjoy the city while you are here! They both smiled as they went different ways.

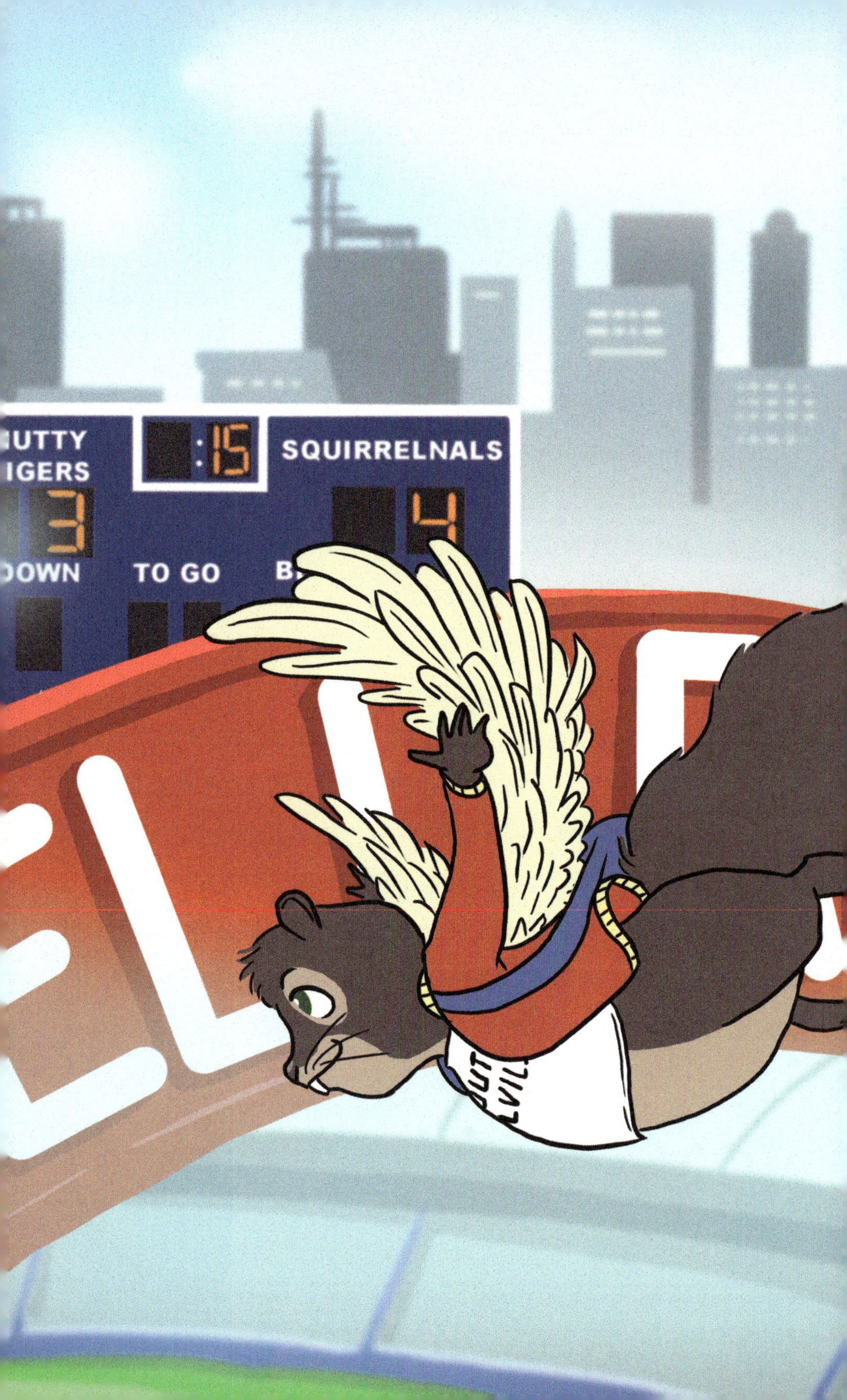
UTTY
IGERS
:15
SQUIRRELNALS
3
4
OWN
TO GO

Bennie passed the scoreboard and the Squirrelnals were beating the Nutty Tigers 4 to 3. He smiled! Flying past the stadium he noticed the Squirrel Arch. That is huge said Bennie. I wonder what it would be like to ride to the top of the arch? He flew into the center of the arch and looked back as everyone was looking at him. He felt so free to have done that! He was thinking to himself what it would be like to be a bird everyday of his life and just fly. Flying along all he noticed was how fast the vehicles were going down the road . They even had cars with no tops on them. He was so amazed to see such different things because he had never seen such in his life. Bennie only dreamed of this place and seen pictures in magazines. He knew he was getting close to his cousin Vinny because he remembered that Vinny used to talk about the Squirrel Arch. Bennie was getting a little hungry so he decided to come down from the air to the ground.

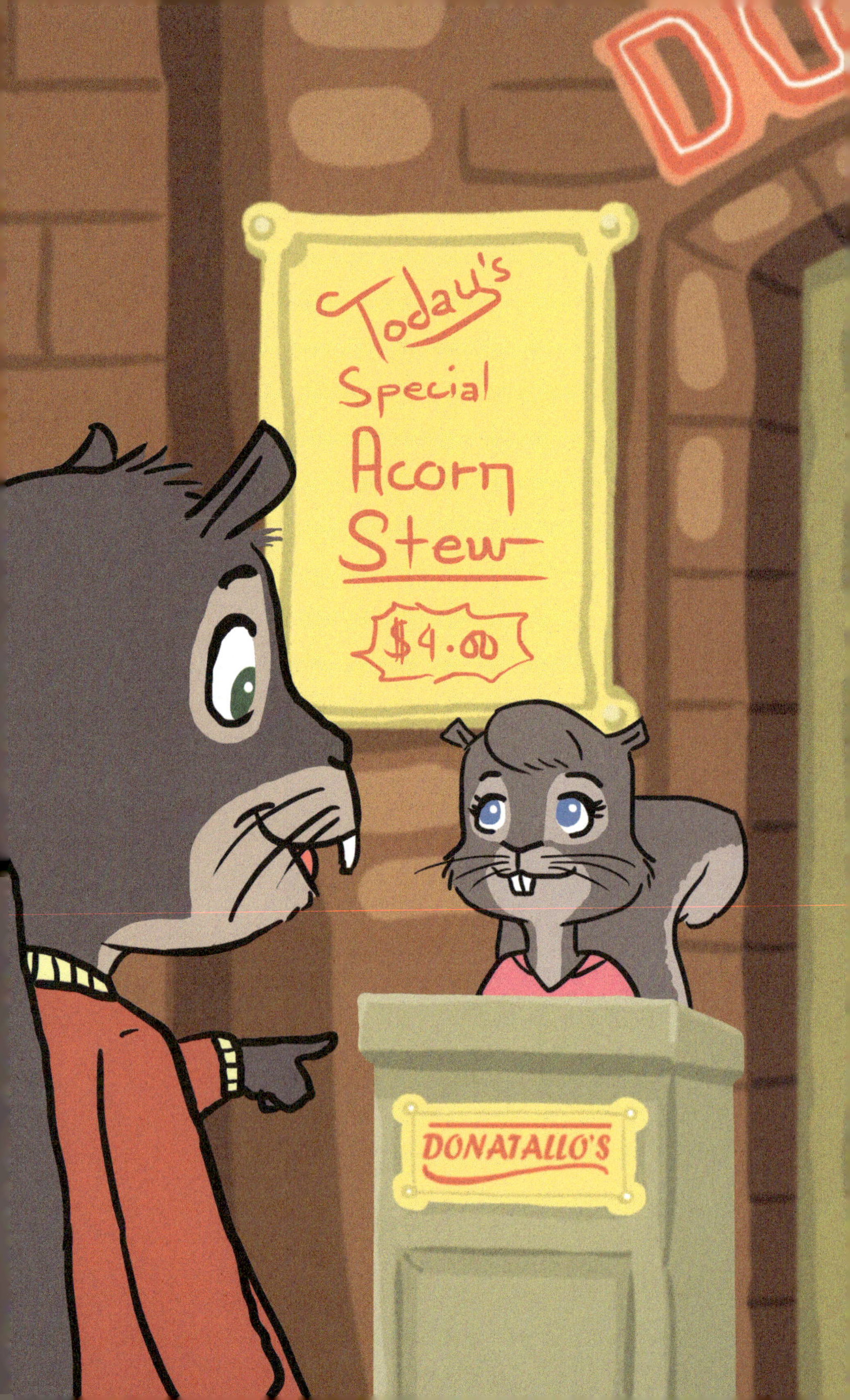
Today's
Special
Acorn
Stew
$4.00
DONATALLO'S

WHEN HE LANDED HE NOTICED THAT THERE WAS A LITTLE ITALIAN RESTAURANT CALLED DONATALLO'S. AS HE WAS WALKING IN BENNIE WAS GREETED AT THE DOOR FROM SOMEONE HE THOUGHT HE KNEW. THEY BOTH LOOKED AT ONE ANOTHER AND SAID, DO I KNOW YOU? BENNIE SAID MY NAME IS BENNIE AND I AM FROM SOUTH SQUIRRELVILLE. THE OTHER SQUIRRELL LOOKED AT HIM FUNNY AND SAID YOUR VINNY'S COUSIN FROM SOUTH SQUIRRELVILLE. WOW! SHE SAID I HAVE HEARD AND SEEN MANY PICTURES OF YOU OVER THE YEARS. MY NAME IS ADRIANNA. BENNIE SAID YOU KNOW MY COUSIN VINNY? WELL YEA SHE SAID! EVERYONE KNOWS HIM. HE IS VERY POPULAR HERE IN THE CITY. AS HE WAS ORDERING THE FOOD. ADRIANNA AND BENNIE WAS TALKING ABOUT WHERE TO FIND HIS COUSIN AT. ADRIANNA SAID SOMETIMES YOU CAN FIND HIM WORKING FOR A MAN NAME MR. DAMICO DOWN BY THE RIVER. IT'S A GREAT PLACE WHERE RICH SQUIRRELS CAN GO SPEND THEIR MONEY AT. BENNIE SAID THANK YOU FOR ALL YOUR HELP! HE FINISHED HIS DINNER AND WENT OUTSIDE TO GO FIND HIS COUSIN VINNY. HE DECIDED TO WALK INSTEAD OF FLYING BECAUSE ADRIANNA SAID IT WAS ONLY TWO BLOCKS AWAY. AS HE WAS WALKING DOWN THE SIDEWALK HE WAS ADMIRING THE CITY AND HOW BRIGHT IT WAS. BENNIE SAID THIS AN AMAZING PLACE! BENNIE GOT CLOSER TO THE BRIGHT LIGHTS. HE NOTICED THAT HE WAS COMING CLOSE TO A SIGN THAT WAS CALLED "THE STAR." WOW! HE SAID! THIS PLACE IS UNBELIEVABLE. HE NOTICED CARS BEING PARKED AND PEOPLE DRESSED UP REAL FANCY. ANOTHER SQUIRREL WITH A RED SUIT CAME UP TO HIM AND SAID CAN I HELP YOU? BENNIE SAID YES. I AM LOOKING FOR A MAN NAMED MR. DAMICO.

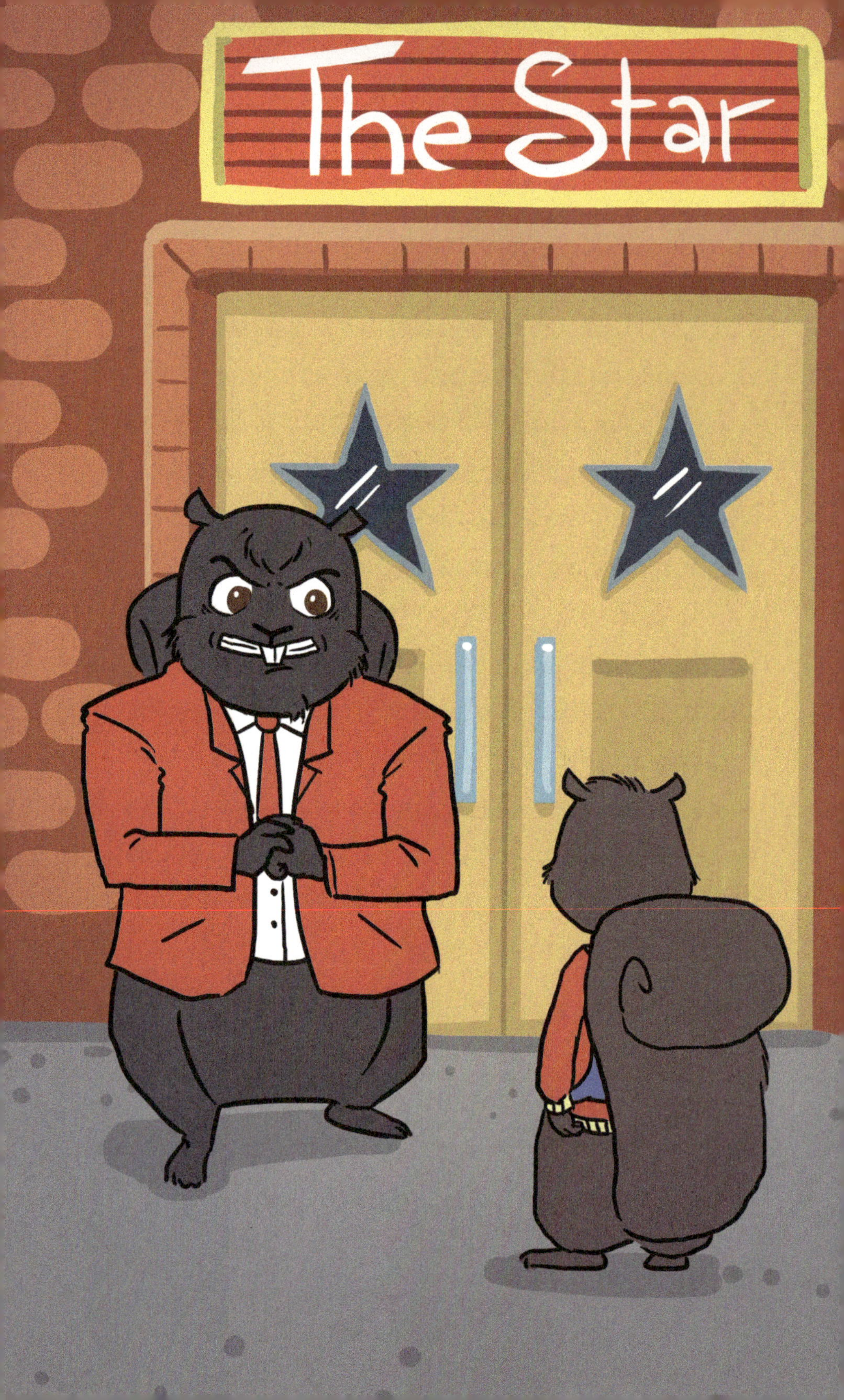
The Star

The squirrel looked at him and said are you sure? Bennie said yes. He might know where my cousin Vinny is at. The squirrel said if I was you, I would leave now because Mr. Damico is a very very powerful man. You do not need to see him. Mr. Damico is bad news. Bennie said to himself, I have traveled this far and I am not leaving without my cousin. So he decided to find Mr. Damico himself. He walked into the fancy place called "The Star" and noticed very expensive chandeliers and restaurants and even a huge water fountain in the middle of the place. Bennie was overwhelmed when he saw the water going straight to the ceiling of the building. He watched squirrels holding hands and even throwing pennies into the water for wishes.

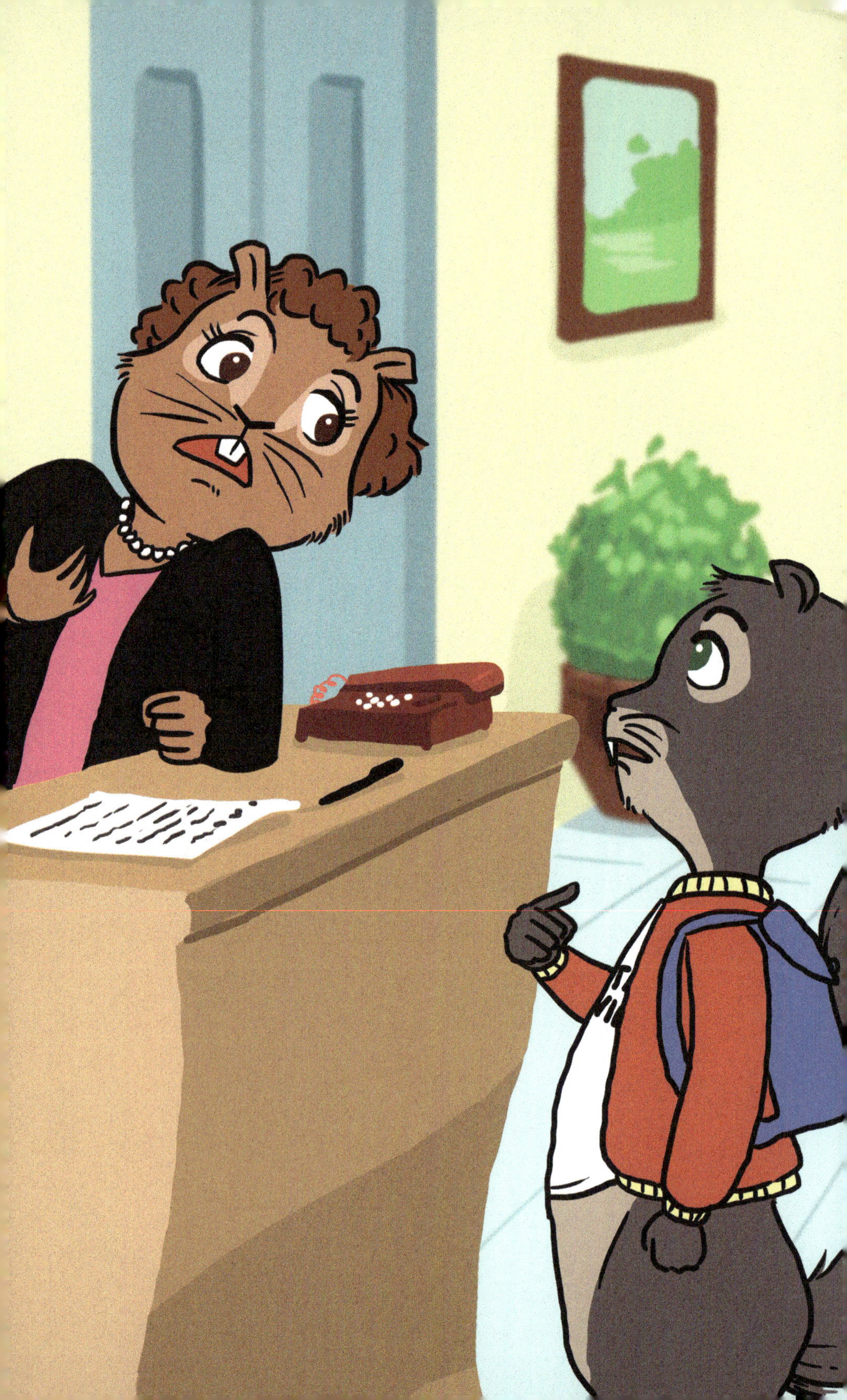

He walked over to the lady at the front desk and asked if he could speak to Mr. Damico. Her eyes got real big and said, do you have an appointment? Bennie said no, but Mr. Damico knows where my cousin Vinny is at. She picked up the phone and called Mr. Damico and told him that Vinny's cousin was here and wanted to speak with him about Vinny. The lady told Bennie that he would have to wait until someone came and got him. Bennie sat down in one of the chairs to wait. A few minutes later Bennie was approached by two of the biggest squirrels that he had ever seen before. Bennie's eyes got big and he got up and followed them to the elevator to the 12th floor where he met Mr. Damico. As he walked into the place he noticed that everything was made out of gold. He had never seen anything like that before and he was very nervous. Mr. Damico introduced himself to Bennie and said hello my name is Mr. Damico but you can call me Tony the Snake.

BENNIE'S FACE GOT RED AND HE WENT TO GO SIT DOWN TO TALK TO MR. DAMICO. TONY THE SNAKE REINSURED BENNIE TO NOT JUDGE A BOOK BY ITS COVER. HE SAID, I AM A VERY BIG SQUIRREL BUT THAT DOES NOT MEAN THAT I AM A MEAN PERSON. BENNIE SAID GOOD, I AM RELIEVED. I AM LOOKING FOR MY COUSIN VINNY. TONY THE SNAKE SAID, YOUR COUSIN VINNY IS IN TROUBLE. BENNIE SAID WHY? WHERE IS HE? TONY THE SNAKE SAID, PAULIE THE FOX KIDNAPED HIM BECAUSE I HAD HIM DELIVER SOME CHANDELIERS FOR HIS HOUSE AND VINNY LIED ABOUT BREAKING THEM. PAULIE THE FOX WILL NOT LET HIM GO UNTIL SOMEONE BRINGS HIM 10,000.00 PIECES OF FRUIT AND FISH. BENNIE SAID WOW! WHAT AM I GOING TO DO? I COME FROM A FAMILY WHO DOES NOT HAVE A WHOLE LOT OF MONEY. HE TOOK HIS HAND AND PLACED IT IN HIS POCKET TO SEE HOW MUCH MONEY HE HAD. HE PULLED OUT A FEW DOLLARS AND LOOKED AT TONY THE SNAKE WITH A FROWN ON HIS FACE. THIS IS ALL I HAVE BENNIE SAID.

TONY THE SNAKE TOLD BENNIE, ILL PAY FOR THIS IF YOU DO ONE THING FOR ME. BENNIE SAID ANYTHING! TONY SAID WHEN I GET TIRED OF THE CITY, I WOULD LIKE TO BRING MY FAMILY TO THE COUNTRY AND SPEND SOME QUALITY TIME WITH THEM. BENNIE SAID ANYTIME! THEY BOTH SMILED AT EACH OTHER AND SHOOK ON IT WITH THEIR HANDS. THEY PUT ALL THE FISH AND FRUIT IN THE BACK OF THE TRUCK AND WENT TO SEE PAULIE THE FOX TO EXCHANGE THE FISH AND FRUIT FOR VINNY. THEY HAD TO DRIVE OVER 100 MILES TO GET THERE. IN THAT TIME THEY TALKED ABOUT LIFE AND FAMILY AND WHAT THEY HAVE ENJOYED OUT OF IT. AS THEY WERE APPROACHING TO THE PLACE, THEY CAME ACROSS THE ENTRANCE WITH FIVE GUARDS AT THE GATE. BENNIE SAID WOW, THEY ARE HUGE!! TONY SAID JUST BE QUIET, I GOT THIS.

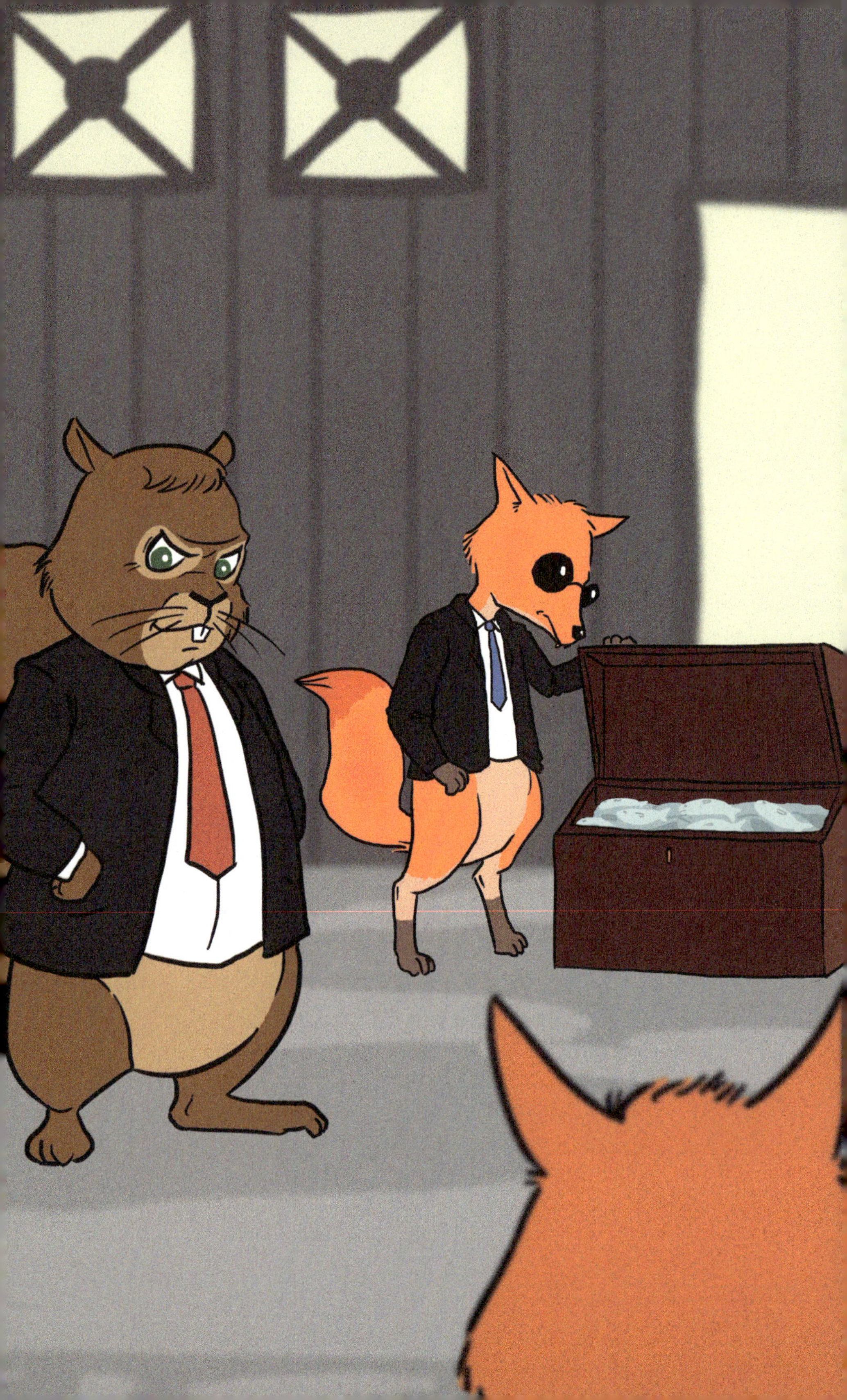

THEY OPENED THE GATES AND PARKED AND PAULIE THE FOX CAME OUT WITH VINNY. THE GUARDS WERE HUGE SQUIRRELS WHO WERE VERY MEAN LOOKING. PAULIE SAID, YOU HAVE MY FISH AND FRUIT? TONY AND BENNIE BOTH REPLIED YES! CAN WE JUST EXCHANGE THEM FOR VINNY? PAULIE SAID YES UNDER ONE CONDITION. BENNIE SAID ANYTHING. WHAT IS IT?

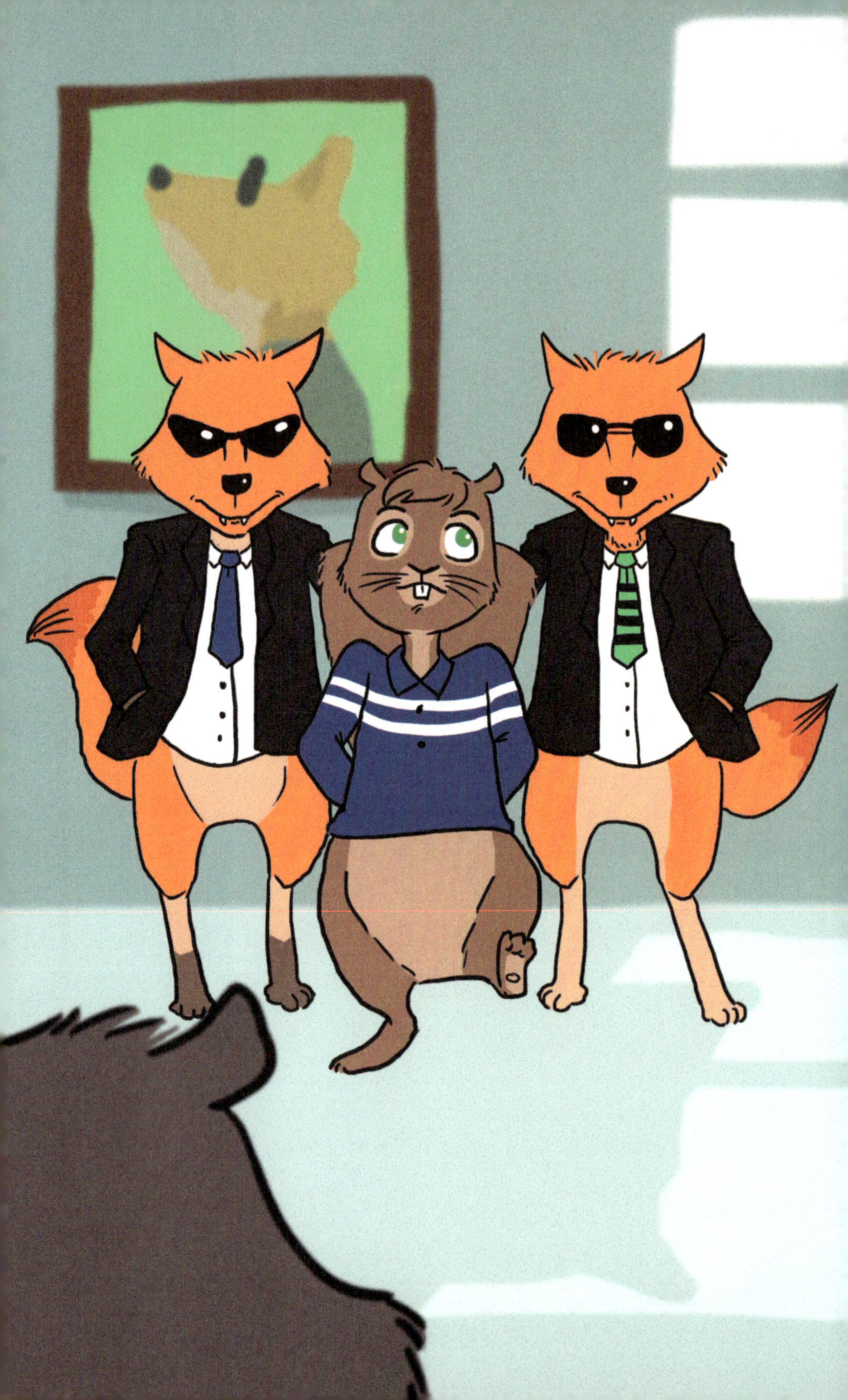

PAULIE SAID THAT VINNY CAN NOT COME BACK TO THE CITY ANYMORE BECAUSE OF WHAT HE DID. BENNIE SAID NO PROBLEM HE WILL COME HOME WITH ME. VINNY GOT INTO THE TRUCK AND THEY ALL LEFT TOGETHER. EVERYONE WAS REAL QUIET FOR A WHILE. THEY JUST NEEDED TO GET BACK TO THE CITY. THEY GOT DOWN THE ROAD AND BENNIE TOLD VINNY THAT THE CITY WAS NOT A GOOD PLACE FOR HIM RIGHT NOW AND THAT HE NEEDED TO COME HOME TO SOUTH SQUIRRELVILLE. VINNY AGREED THAT THE CITY WAS TOO DANGEROUS FOR HIM BECAUSE OF WHAT HE DID. VINNY SAID I DO LOVE IT HERE BUT I UNDERSTAND THAT THE CITY IS NOT WHERE I NEED TO BE RIGHT NOW. IT IS TOO DANGEROUS. THEY GOT BACK TO "THE STAR" AND BENNIE SAID THANK YOU SO MUCH FOR HELPING US OUT TONY! TONY THE SNAKE SAID I WILL SEE YOU SOON WITH MY FAMILY. BENNIE SAID, MY HOME IS YOUR HOME. YOU AND YOUR FAMILY ARE WELCOME ANYTIME. BENNIE AND VINNY TALKED AND TALKED THAT NIGHT AND THEY BOTH AGREED THAT THIS WAS THE RIGHT THING TO DO.

CRAFTS

THE NEXT MORNING BENNIE AND VINNY WENT TO GO FIND SOME FEATHERS TOGETHER SO VINNY WOULD HAVE SOME WINGS TO FLY BACK TO SOUTH SQUIRRELVILLE. THEY FOUND SOME WINGS AT A LOCAL FARM STORE AND BENNIE ASKED VINNY, ARE YOU READY? VINNY SAID I HAVE ALWAYS BEEN READY! I AM READY TO GO HOME AND FIND MY ROOTS AGAIN! THEY SMILED AT ONE ANOTHER AND STARTED FLYING TOGETHER IN THE AIR TO GO BACK HOME TO SOUTH SQUIRRELVILLE.

THE END

e|LIVE

listen|imagine|view|experience

AUDIO BOOK DOWNLOAD INCLUDED WITH THIS BOOK!

In your hands you hold a complete digital entertainment package. In addition to the paper version, you receive a free download of the audio version of this book. Simply use the code listed below when visiting our website. Once downloaded to your computer, you can listen to the book through your computer's speakers, burn it to an audio CD or save the file to your portable music device (such as Apple's popular iPod) and listen on the go!

How to get your free audio book digital download:

1. Visit www.tatepublishing.com and click on the e|LIVE logo on the home page.
2. Enter the following coupon code:
   1e37-c122-260e-1c8c-a82a-b9af-6526-27df
3. Download the audio book from your e|LIVE digital locker and begin enjoying your new digital entertainment package today!